NOW THEN

Dearest Mum,

Hope this is an
inspiration...

love

Vera.

crocus

c r o c u s

NOW THEN

A Celebration
of Changing Times
in Poetry and Stories

First published in 1989 by Crocus

Crocus books are published by
Commonword Ltd,
Cheetwood House,
21 Newton Street,
Manchester M1 1FZ.

Commonword gratefully acknowledges financial assistance from the Association of Greater Manchester Authorities, North West Arts Association and Manchester City Council.

Typeset and printed by Rap Ltd, Rochdale, OL12 7AF.

Cover photograph courtesy of Maureen Tottoh.

British Library Cataloguing in Publication Data

Now Then.
1. English literature. Special subjects.
England. North-West. Social life, 1945-1988.
Anthologies
820.8'032427

ISBN 0 946745 55 2

Contents

Foreword

These stories and poems reflect real life; the life that is rarely available in commercial writing.

Each writer has donated something from a rich store of memories and experiences which will be instantly recognised by the reader as similar to his or her own. Although most of the memories take one back to an age which has passed, the relationships and reactions are timeless.

These contributions to literature belong to the future even though they arise out of the past. There will come a time when the work of ordinary working people is recognised as the highest form of the writer's art. They will be appreciated long after the introspective and idealistic meanderings which too often pass for literature today will have been rejected.

There is nothing complicated in this work. It is straight from the heart, simple and direct. These writers are not special people highly trained and developed. They are writers with a working class background and experience to call upon; and in that lies their strength.

If reading this work inspires others to look into their own life and pull out an episode to write down, the effort will be well worth while. The more such work is produced and published, the richer will be the inheritance of working class literature we shall pass on to future generations.

Ruth and Edmund Frow
The Working Class Movement Library, Salford

Introduction

Now Then is history with a difference. It takes as its starting point 1945, and moves right through to the present day. These poems and stories, written by people from Greater Manchester, show that history is a living process, not simply something that happened 'long, long ago'.

All too quickly things change and whole ways of life disappear. *Now Then* records some of the experiences of the last forty years. We hope it will encourage many more people to write down their own stories and poems, retelling their histories.

There is writing here about homelife, school and work. We also find out what people did to enjoy themselves. Mary James tells us of hours endured in front of the fire, with a head full of kirby grips, in order to look 'just right' for Saturday night at Bury Palais.

Change and continuity is looked at humorously by Maureen Tottoh in 'For Judy'as she laughs with us at the fashions of now and then. Decisions for teenagers have never been easy it seems, as Nell Harwood tells us about Jane who meets up with her teacher again eight years after leaving school. She bitterly regrets having given up full time education to work in the local mill, but feels a sense of loss at the thought of leaving the camaraderie of women and girls there. What will she decide to do now?

Joy Openshaw's family covered their table legs with woolly 'stockings'. Discover why as she takes you through their move to a new council house on a Salford overspill estate in 'A New Life in Little Hulton'. She recalls how their first night there was like staying in a first class hotel. Later on you find out why the secret cache of wild orchids grew on 'Stink bomb hill'.

In 'Home For Whitsun' Sally Dawson fits in a visit to the Hallé in between shopping on Salford market and bathing the local kids in readiness for the wonderful Whit Walks. She scrubs their grimy bodies until they're pink, while older girls dream of becoming 'Cotton Queen' for the year.

In 'Leaving' things are going wrong for a Wythenshawe mum, when a day out with the children isn't such a picnic anymore. Just what is the mysterious parcel in the bottom of the pram?

These are just a small selection from the writing contained in *Now Then*. It's often said that once you start talking about the old days you can't stop. We think that you'll agree that the writers in *Now Then* have a lot to tell us — some who feel that those were 'the good old days', others who welcome the changes that have occurred. The stories and poems you'll find among these pages give a view of the North West not often found in the pages of more traditional history books. These are stories from people's lives, vividly and honestly told, about a critical period in recent history.

We would like to end by recording our thanks to the many members of Commonword workshops who took part in the editorial process, sifting through the enormous amount of work that was submitted for the book.

Liz Rutherford and Helen Windrath

Bury Palais

Mary James

It was just a stark wooden building, painted black standing beside the Bury to Manchester railway line but to the lads and lasses of Bury, for over three decades, 'The Palais' was another world. A world of music and romance if you were lucky...

Anne Bradbury waited in eager anticipation for Saturday night, it was the highlight of her week. The memory of last Saturday and the joy of another on its way, sustained her as she worked at her weaving in the 'Waterside Mill' on the banks of the canal.

The weekend began on Friday night with the ritual of hair washing. 'Friday Night is Amami Night' said the advertisement for a popular brand of shampoo. Anne would wash her hair and put it into curling pins, the shorter ends she would secure into pin clips by criss-crossing a couple of kirby grips. It took all evening to dry by the coal fire in the living room, and Friday night was an endurance test for Anne as she tossed and turned in bed with a head full of metal, but she suffered it all in the safe assurance that her hair would look 'alright' for the Palais.

The Bradburys were lucky, no tin bath by the fire for them. Her father had had a small endowment and invested in a real 'plumbed in' bath. The house had three bedrooms but these were all occupied by family, so ingeniously the bath had been installed in a huge built-in cupboard on the landing. It was luxury! The only snag being if little sister wanted to go to bed in the back bedroom, she had to walk through the cupboard the doors of which had been brought forward to accommodate the bath, so dreams of Saturday night had to be curtailed as Anne jumped for the towel and opened the door to let the little one through.

Saturday had a special air about it, after shopping for Mum on Bury market, Anne would eat her tea to the sounds of the football results coming over the walnut radio in the corner as Dad eagerly checked his pools for the fortune he was sure he would win one day.

Then it was time. The excitement would begin as she went upstairs to get ready. What would she wear tonight? Her mother had made her a new taffetta blouse, blue with a Chinese-style mandarin collar, she would wear this with her black swirling skirt.

Every week the routine was the same, she met her friend Josie outside Jeanette's, the dress shop in Bolton Street, sheltering in the doorway if it rained. Eagerly they would cross the road, over a dirt track, and enter the beloved portals.

The strains of Jack Hawkin's band welcomed them and set their hearts dancing as they paid to go in.

Into the cloakroom first, where in front of the wall to wall mirrors the cream of Bury's young lasses would be found, applying their mascara and rouge. A last look to be sure all was well, then into the fray.

There was always a preponderance of females in the dance hall at first, the young men of Bury were still in the Napier Inn, or the Old Boar or the Lord Nelson, buying Dutch courage at 1/3d per pint. Nevertheless it was a happy atmosphere as the girls awaited 10.30 pm and the exodus of their anticipated partners from the pubs.

All eyes were on the door as each young female waited for her current heart-throb and hoped he would arrive before the 'Ladies' Choice'.

The highlight of the evening was the 'Top Ten' when the ten most popular tunes that week were played. No matter what rhythm the tune was, everyone moved in exactly the same way around the overcrowded floor. It was a sort of shuffle, shuffle round the floor but if you were in the arms of a current love, the experience was bliss!

Anne would wait eagerly for the man of the moment to arrive and after a few dances to hear the immortal words 'Can I take you home?' If he had a good reputation she would accept and after a goodnight cuddle round the back of the terraced row in which she lived, would perhaps make arrangements to go in the pictures on Sunday.

There were seven picture-houses at that time in the town each competing for custom. The Art used a gimmick where before the film started a singsong would ensue, with the words of the song flashed up on the screen and a little white ping- pong ball would dance along the words to help with the tempo.

The back row of the cinema would be occupied by the more 'forward' young couples, who didn't really care about watching the film but were more interested in kissing and cuddling.

Anne would never sit on the back row and a cautious holding of hands was all she would permit.

After the pictures, the bus stops around Kay Gardens would be bustling with people. Anne's parents insisted that she should be home by 11 pm on Sunday, nobody decent would want to be out after that, and anyway she had to be up early for her shift at the mill.

Going Back On The Irwell

Ron Redshaw

Sometimes, a sound, a sight or even a particular odour can trigger off in our minds the memories of a time long since passed. Happy times, sad times, tragic times. They are all retained, stored in the hidden corners of the mind forever. For me, yesterday became 1957. It was a warm day in June as I strolled alongside the River Irwell in Salford. I stopped and leaned on the newly erected steel safety rail. As I gazed down at the deceptively clean looking water something caught my eye — a dropping from a passing pigeon!

I love the River Irwell. In its own way it is quite unique. It has a smell all of its own, especially on a warm day like yesterday.

Once, in 1956, I sat by a mountain stream in North Wales. I sat on a rock not five yards from the water. What could I smell? Nothing but the trees and grass. Standing up here, at least fifty yards from the water, what could I smell? Filth! Not your everyday common or garden filth, but unique filth, mega multiple nose bashing filth. No matter, I still love the Irwell.

Sometimes, in high summer, I would deliberately catch a cold so that I could spend an inoffensive day by the River Irwell and thank God for not giving us the power to see smells.

I once read in the press that someone had reported seeing a heron on the Salford end of the Irwell. A heron! Not only did he see a heron but he also said that it had a fish in its beak. A fish? In the River Irwell? Surely there must be some mistake. Perhaps it was a long-legged rat chewing on a sardine can. Still, I suppose people will see what they want to see despite us cynics. I saw a reindeer on the banks of the Irwell a long time ago. I didn't report it to the press mind. On closer inspection it turned out to be a totter's horse which had escaped from a nearby field. It was stripping the leaves from the branches of a shrub. That's what fooled me, the branches.

When I was a kid, the Irwell was a good place to hide. I often spent many happy hours exploring the make-believe jungle which I had created on its banks. In those days they were a mass of wild flowers and trees, skirting the river like brightly coloured garlands. Now the banks are nothing more than sloping concrete and closely cropped grass. God bless the town planners — they sorted it out. I appreciate their concern for our safety and the river is very unpredictable. Who knows? Maybe it will burst its banks again just like it did in 1866. Best stop its nonsense now, just in case.

The river was calm yesterday, peaceful. Gliding by on its way to the sea. Rippling through wires of reed captured supermarket trolleys and suspicious looking tied sacks. A dog barking on the opposite bank brings back a memory from when I was twelve years old. A friend and me saved a dog from drowning in the Irwell. It was splashing about in the middle barking for help. We quickly launched our lifeboat and paddled like mad towards the helpless creature, shouting words of encouragement. When we finally reached it, the ungrateful beast refused to be pulled in. In fact, the stupid thing capsized the boat, and we found ourselves up to our waists in stinking black water. Half the lifeboat sank and the other half just stuck up in the air like a lopsided gravestone. Still, we managed to save the dog despite his protests. We dragged him out and sent him on his way with a good scolding.

When I got home my dad half killed me. Funny that. I never knew you could get half killed. I always thought it had to be all or nothing. And to top it all, that damned dog was back in the water next day. Not drowning, but swimming, just like the day before.

Another thing I remember about the Irwell was the poppies. Hundreds of different coloured poppies growing in clusters all along the banks. They got opium from poppies. That's what I was told. My friend and me were smart, very sharp and so clever. What did we do? We gathered bunches of petals, rolled them up in white bus tickets and smoked them. We were sick! Surely people didn't pay money to smoke stuff like that, I thought. Anyway, afterwards, we were convinced that we were now drug addicts and that was the end of that.

Speaking of flowers reminds me of the bee farm. One of a million get rich quick schemes for which my friend and me were famous. Never rich, just famous. Everyday the Irwell was swarming with bees. The most popular flower was a little red one that hung over like a tiny tulip. The bees had to go right inside the flower to get at the pollen which meant that they could not see us. That was their first mistake, the rest were made by us. We found a rusty old biscuit tin and covered the top with a sheet of glass. That was our hive. All we had to do now was catch our bees. Simple! We each got a jam jar and a small piece of cardboard, waited for a bee to enter a flower and presto! one captured honey maker plus flower-head.

About twenty five bees later we sat watching them confused in the biscuit tin. Half an hour passed, no honey! An hour, still no honey! The swines were refusing to co-operate. This was their revenge for being taken prisoner. After a while — and not because we were bloody fed up — we decided to show them that there were no hard feelings and let them go. I got stung twice, ouch! ouch! Contemptible insects! That was my thanks for giving them a good home.

Still, I forgive them, that was a long time ago. I've grown up now. I know that opium doesn't come from poppy petals and when I see a lifeboat in the river, well, it's just a tin bath. That's it then. It's 1989 again and I'm feeling tired. Funny that, in those days I never got tired. Still, I enjoyed yesterday, going back on the Irwell.

New Sounds For Old

John Rankle

I stood at the end of the street, remembering that it was many, many years since my last visit. My immediate impression was that the road appeared surprisingly unchanged. The terraced houses, built some fifty-odd years before, had retained the smooth, unweathered shine of red Accrington bricks. The garden walls topped with solid curving tiles reflected the same enduring quality, and the evergreen privets still shielded the modest gardens from public gaze.

There are still in the Oldham area many such streets that have escaped the all-consuming bulldozer, and appeared also to have resisted the eruption of change.

Naturally change, sometimes under the questionable guise of progress, had evolved even in this urban backwater. The contrasting brightness of paintwork over gutters, doors and sills, so revolutionary from the dull, conforming greens and browns of former years.

Perhaps only an experienced decorator would have been aware of the regrettable decline in the number of finely grained doors. Certainly a woman would have noticed the rich draperies of the draw curtains that, so long ago, initially replaced the discreet netted curtains and secretive Venetian blinds.

I was aware of the cars in this once cobbled street, and knew that later in the day, many more cars would be parked along its length. I remembered as a boy, the same spectacle of four cars closely parked in the street.

They were black gleaming limousines, the first being a hearse and I recall the stifling sadness that hung over the street. In the magnificent isolation of its quietly purring journey to the cemetery, the funeral procession was seen as an impressive though tragic exit from life. Today such journeys are less noticed as the cortege soon becomes lost in the congestion of traffic.

Along with the visual change wrought by time and progress there is the accompaniment of new sounds replacing the old. Road traffic today dominates all other sounds and at peak time even subdues the noise of aircraft straying across our local sky. By comparison the street sounds of yesteryear evoke more pleasant connotations.

In my tender years both dinner-time and tea-time were signified by the sudden clattering of clogs worn by homeward bound cotton operatives. Clogs were acceptable footwear in those days and their distinctive sounds constant-ly reverberated in our streets.

The clear resonant rhythm of girls skipping in unison to age-old chants, was a delightful sound that the soft shoe skipping of today's children fails dismally to emulate.

There were the personal identifiable cries of the street traders. Yet I could never quite spell out the whole of the traders' vocal inducements and to this day I am intrigued by the ragman's cry of 'rag a bone'. Maybe in the past, bones were bartered for but I never witnessed such a transaction. The cobbled streets rang to the occasional beat of horses' hooves, and to the rumble of carts. Today we have the incessant buzz of cars and the nerve fraying roar of heavy transport.

There was no mistaking in my youth the thrilling sound of the fire-engine, though I regretted never once hearing the authentic blast of a policeman's whistle . Now we have with confusing frequency, the sirens of police cars, ambulance, or was it the fire-engine?

The shrill, sopranic pipings of newsboys and the sentimental 'airs'of street singers and buskers have long been disciplined from our streets. I remember one singer, a limbless victim of World War One. He would proceed slowly along the gutter, singing his ballads. He never begged at any door but relied hopefully on the streets' inhabitants, generally children to emerge and shyly drop coins in his proffered cap. Another musical offering was the omnipresent thumping of pianos in the early evenings, often complemented by the sight of the youthful musicians rebelliously practising their scales on front room pianos.

Less frequent were the sounds of accordians and banjos but for obvious reasons the humble mouth organ was the authentic musical voice of the street. At a certain time each year an accompaniment to the harmonica uncannily re-emerged. It was the castanet-like sound of rickers. Rickers was the name given to a pair of animal rib bones, previously obtained from the butcher, the ends burned clean and the rickers then ground and polished. They were held by the fingers and manipulated by the wrist to produce the repetitve clicking sound.

Pieces of slate cut to a convenient length were effective substitutes. Today's street music blares forth effortlessly from the transistor sets of teenagers ambling down the roads. Television is a dominating factor in our lives and rivals even our unpredictable weather as an endless source of discussion. It is possible to walk the length of a street and hear the continuity of a programme from house to house.

On certain nights the quietest of streets may be shattered by the criss-cross gun shots of the Virginians. Caught mentally unprepared, one's impulsive reaction is a compelling urge to crouch low beneath the garden walls to ensure a safe and bloodless conduct of one's journey.

The old street gas lamp was the focal centre of noisy activity during those winter evenings. It was the Den — an oasis of lights creating and illuminating the street's own open-air Youth Club.

Unlike the coldly remote electric standards of today the gas lamps with their continuous snake-like hissing and flickering glow simulated a cosy feeling of warmth. We took for granted that the design and structure of the lamp was primarily to enable us to develop our acrobatic skills. During respites from our winter games, adventurous ones would 'shindy'up the lamp, sometimes to light an illicit cigarette from the wavering flame, or hang bat-like from the convenient arm. As a child drowsily awaiting sleep, I often heard the melancholy whistle of a steam train. Occasionally too, I would hear the weird cry of a barn owl from a nearby farm, which, like the railroad has long been obliterated. Those days held many periods of natural quiet yet I remember particularly the officially created silence on a certain November 11th. The piercing drawn-out shriek of a factory hooter descended upon the street. All movement froze and I was aware of the intense silence that followed. Street vendors stood solemnly by their horses and carts. A few shawl-covered housewives, caught between home and shop, stood in quiet meditation and a small group of workmen came awkwardly to attention. Beyond this silent street my young mind envisaged a greater awesome silence reaching out to unite and encompass the whole wide world.

For Judy (1962)

Maureen Tottoh

Today I saw two girls on Market Street,
Heads bent forward as they walked against
                                    the wind.
Swaying and clutching at each other as they
                                    laughed.
Spiked hair with stripes of pink and green,
Long black skirts and leather boots,
With bits of rag criss-crossed around their
                                    legs.

And I thought of you and me, linking
With the collars of our double-breasted Wallis
                                    coats
Turned up (the fashion rather than the cold).
Back-combed hair, lacquered till it didn't feel
                                    like hair,
Winkle-picker shoes and hobble skirts
Tilting us forward on tiny steps.
C & A bags swinging from our hands,
Carrying a dream for less than thirty bob.
Laughing as we talked about the Ritz last
                                    night,
Tears streaming as you told me what he said.
And home to paint our nails with pearly
                                    peach.

John Willie Greaves

Harry Crossley

John Willie Greaves wandered slowly through the gates of the mill yard, then stopped, and turned round.

'So that's it then, the end of my working life. Not a bad age to retire at, sixty, generous compensation too. Fancy that, actually being paid *not* to work.'

Gazing up at the massive, solid brick structure, he was aware of the unusual silence surrounding the mill, a silence that for the past seventy years had occurred only once a year, for one week of the Wakes holidays when the engineers cleaned the boilers and overhauled the machinery.

Yes John Willie, that's it. On Monday the fitters will be here to start stripping out the complex, beautifully created looms and weaving machines. Aye, something about sending it all abroad to equip a mill out there.

Forty six years, working full time in there, only four minutes walk from the little terraced house where he lived alone. Quite often, in the past few years, he had wondered what it would have been like to work somewhere else. But no, he reflected, it wouldn't have been any different. They all make the same thing, pay the same wages, work the same hours, and have the same holidays. Why, at Wakes Week in Blackpool or the Isle of Man it was home from home. He'd certainly never forget the sight of fifteen stone Nellie Turner paddling in the sea with the hem of her frock tucked into the legs of her bloomers. But the people had a different air about them on holiday, an air of gay abandonment. They left behind them the cares and routines of the mill, meal making, washing and mending, and handed themselves over to the boarding house landladies. By heck, the wives enjoyed that, having their meals made for them, their beds made for them, no washing up for a whole week.

He sighed as a familiar memory flitted through his head, a memory of strolling along the prom arm in arm with Florrie. Their two daughters having taken it into their heads to get married in the previous twelve months, this was the first holiday they'd had on their own in all their married life. And how they'd appreciated each others' company, how peaceful everything seemed. They seemed to draw closer together, without the distractions of noisy children, or the physical or mental exhaustion after a day's work. Their love for each other reached a further stage in its development in the way that love progresses through various stages in a marriage.

They planned the next year's holiday in the Isle of Man. John Willie's mouth tightened bitterly; Florrie clung to that planned holiday up to the very day she died, three weeks before they were to have gone.

John Willie turned his tall, gaunt frame to go up the street, but the thought of going into that empty house stopped him. No, things are different now old lad, the routine of forty odd years is finished. I can come and go as I please, if I please. A heaviness seemed to bow his angular shoulders. 'My God, what am I going to do with myself, day after day, month after month?'

Turning on his heel, he stretched his long legs and shiny size ten boots over the cracked flagstones and headed for the little park at the bottom of the street. This tiny green oasis surrounded by a forest of mill chimneys seemed, somehow out of place. What had prompted the planners to preserve this three acres, when, in the mad old days cotton mills were being scattered over the landscape like confetti? John Willie and his pals had often ruminated on this question in the tap room. Whatever the answer, they were all grateful for it; the bowling greens always did a good trade in the summer.

As he passed through the wrought iron gates he lifted his head and sniffed the air. 'Yes, it's there, the smell of freshly cut grass, flowers, never-ending evergreens. You know, coming through those gates is like passing through the gates of heaven.'

Everything shone in the warm evening sunlight, and the click of the woods on the greens generated a feeling of subdued excitement. Voices floated across to him, checking a score, good humoured banter, then a voice raised in a shout.

'Hey John Willie, what are you doing here at this time o' day, shouldn't you be home getting your tea on?'

'Naw, not tonight Billy, things are different now.'

'Oh aye, mill closes today doesn't it? Perhaps we'll see more of you down here then.'

John Willie's eyes wandered over the scene, then came to rest on the small wooden building on the far side of the greens.

'Well well, the veterans' hut, is that my next move? There's old Alf, Jacob and Isaac, they're all in their seventies. Still, time won't stand still for me, and if I live to their age I expect I'll be only too glad to go and park on that bench. Bandy Bill there is still active and he's been retired — on the pension that is — for three years. Grand chap though is Billy, such a pity he's so bowlegged; usual story, rickets as a youngster, common disease in the old days. And a wonderful sense of humour; had to have in his condition. He always says you can drive a carriage and pair through his legs without touching the sides; and loves cricket but makes a lousy stumper. Then his crony Tommy Farrar rounds off the double act with 'he couldn't stop a pig in a ginnel'. No, not a bad crowd really.'

Yes, the sun is definitely much hotter in Lancashire than it used to be. Stands to reason doesn't it? It doesn't have to fight its way through a thick blanket of smoke and grime to get to us. By gum, the closures of all these cotton mills, and bringing in all these smokeless zones has transformed the place. And it needed it! These days we have different shades of green; it used to be different shades of grey. Why, on a so-called sunny day you could look directly at the sun, it was just a glowing ball with no real strength.

John Willie placed his lunch box on one of the green painted benches and sat down beside it, folded his arms, crossed his legs and leaned back. This was something he really enjoyed, but it was usually on a Saturday or Sunday when he had an odd hour to spare. This warm evening mellowness was a new experience to him. But a vague uneasiness crept over him — something he couldn't quite put his finger on. Was it this change in his way of life, this having to consider changing the habits of a lifetime? And a creature of habit was our John Willie. Liked to know just where he stood. Oh he'd known this early retirement was coming, they'd known for months that the mill was closing down, but, he hadn't wanted to face it, kept shoving it to the back of his mind.

Should have made plans, got some sort of job lined up; but he couldn't see himself as a lollipop man, or sweeping up in some engineering shop.

He smiled to himself as he recalled the conversations they'd had in the lunch breaks, about the solid construction of the mills, the lift towers, and walls in some places several feet thick of good Accrington brick. The verdict was always the same as they put down their empty mugs.

'Oh aye, they built 'em to last in the old days.'

'I suppose you'll be spending your time with your daughters now then?'

John Willie opened his eyes with a start, suddenly aware that he had been dozing, and found the watery stare of Isaac fixed upon him.

'Yes, yes I suppose so Isaac,' he replied, at the same time conscious of the fact that he'd never considered the question.

'Well it's alright for you with families,' there was a slightly peevish note in Isaac's voice, 'I have nobody you know.'

John Willie stared back at him, feeling irritable enough not to answer. He knew Isaac had never been married, so what did he expect? Batchelors, what did they know? What did they know about the heartaches and heartbreaks, and the joys of bringing up a family? What did they know about the kind of life where a man's every thought, every action was planned for the well-being of others — his family? A kind of life where, when everyone else was taken care of, Dad could come along and perhaps see if there was anything he could get out of life. A life of left-overs. One thing was certain, being a parent didn't leave much room for selfishness.

The old man went on his way but he had left a new line of thought in John Willie's head.

'Yes of course, why not? I'll spend a few days with our Irene in Lytham. They're always asking me why I don't go over. After all, time means nothing to me now, and I could get to know the grandchildren much better. Good lad is her David, got his head screwed on the right way. Not what you'd call a dynamic sort of chap at all, but a plodder. Well, I've never heard of an accountant short of two ha'pennies to rub togther. They might not be as loaded as our Joan and her Ian — well not yet anyway — but they'll get on, of that I've no doubt.

That Ian, I just don't know what to make of him. They certainly don't seem short of money; posh house in Hazel Grove, white poodle and a caravan in Anglesey. There must be something in second-hand car dealing. As far as I can see he just tarts up old bangers and sells 'em to the mugs as he calls 'em. What he really means is he sells 'em to ordinary working class chaps who've just scraped enough together to get a cheap car.'

John Willie stared over the tops of the trees

fringing the bowling greens, to where one boundary of the park was formed by one wall of the adjacent mill. He found that wall both depressing and beautiful at the same time. Even though a gigantic brick wall could be a depressing sight, he could not help but feel admiration for those massive and solid looking ledges and buttresses of that construction.

'Aye, they built 'em to last in the old days.'

His eye moved on to the next mill down the line. This one was closed down twelve months ago and was half demolished, the site littered with bulldozers and cranes. There was one machine standing amid a pile of rubble and whole, one ton blocks of masonry torn off those ledges and buttresses that John Willie had been admiring. From the end of the sixty foot jib dangled a half ton iron ball, poised over a ragged, broken section of the mill wall.

Can you see it John Willie? It's just waiting for morning, so that it can begin again, smashing pounding at that wall. Within a very short time it will be as if that mill never existed at all. And what of all those people who poured through those gates on a Monday morning, grey faced and silent, to come pouring out on a Friday evening, clutching their pay packets, chattering and laughing. Well it will be just as if they never existed either.

No John Willie, nothing lasts, nothing at all.

John Willie Goes Home

Harry Crossley

John Willie sat on the edge of the bed, waiting not so patiently for his daughter Irene and her husband to come and take him home from the hospital. He wouldn't be sorry to go home, no, he loved his home, old-fashioned though it may be; it contained all that he owned in this life. More than that, it contained the memories of the happiest times of his life.

Even so, he had no complaints about his treatment in the hospital; on the contrary, he must admit, he had been looked after really well. Some of those nurses, by gum, they're right rum little devils, but they do like a laugh and joke and they certainly know how to cheer a man up. Well, a hospital could soon become a morbid pile of bricks and mortar with all that sickness and death around it.

'Yes,' thought John Willie, 'I have a lot of respect and admiration for these lasses, they have to work really hard to qualify in this kind of a job; and the things they have to do for some of the patients. By gum, it really is a — what do they call it? Aye, a vocation.'

The ward door swung open suddenly, and

John Willie half rose from the bed before he realised it was Marion, one of the nurses. She came through, bustling and rustling busily, arms full of pillow cases, a big beaming smile on her round plump face. Plopping the linen down on the bed she pinched John Willie's cheek and said, 'Right dad, now when you get out of here I want you to take it easy, just relax, and remember, no chasing ladies round the settee.'

'Chance would be a fine thing,' he replied, then immediately felt embarrassed and a little surprised at himself for talking in this manner, for John Willie had always been a little old-fashioned when it came to relationships between the sexes. Even though Florrie had been gone now for some years, for some strange reason he had a nagging little feeling of guilt whenever he considered an association with another female.

'Come off it dad,' she boomed heartily, 'a handsome chap like you should have no trouble getting a girlfriend.' She pounded the pillow then moved round to the other side of the bed, nudging him off his perch as she did so. '(Move your bum,' she said, 'I've got to get this bed ready for the next patient.'

He moved across the ward and gazed out of the window, across the lawns and flower beds, at the rows of trees, young and old, for the most part bare of leaves; just an occasional brown leaf fluttered to the ground. The sky was overcast with varying hues of silver and dark grey, threatening rain. On the far side of the trees he could just make out the little park where he went bowling, and beyond that the towering bulk of the mill where he had spent all his working life.

Then Marion's hearty voice broke in upon his reverie.

'Wake up dad, they've come to take you away.' He turned to see Irene and David walking down the ward towards him; but there was something wrong, the expressions on their faces told him they were troubled. They glanced at one another as they stopped in front of him.

'What's up?' he said, 'you two don't look very pleased with yourselves.'

'Sit down dad,' Irene took his elbow and steered him to a chair. John Willie was beginning to feel uneasy. He looked at David who was nervously adjusting his glasses, looking like a short-sighted walrus with his droopy moustache and fat little cheeks.

'Yes dad, sit down,' added David.

'What's up,' repeated John Willie, 'what's wrong? Are the children alright, nothing's happened to them has it?'

'No dad no, they're perfectly alright.' Irene paused briefly then went on in something of a rush as if she didn't know how to say it so let the words tumble out. 'It's your house, somebody's broken the back window.'

'Oh. Well that's nowt to get a sweat on about, I've had my back window broken before now.'

David now took up the story, 'Well there's more to it than that, you see they got inside.'

' 'You mean I've been burgled, is that what you're trying to say?'

'Yes dad. When we got here from Lytham this morning we called round at your house to get things ready for your homecoming, and found everything tipped up. We've tidied up as best we can, but we don't know what's missing. You'll have to sort that out; the police have been, and they're coming back later.'

'My radio,' said John Willie suddenly, 'did you see my radio?'

'No,' said David, 'where do you usually keep it?'

'On top of the sideboard, wasn't it there?' There was a note of alarm in his voice.

'Well I didn't see it,' answered Irene, 'all the drawers had been emptied over the floor, and we put all that back, a bit mixed up perhaps but it's off the floor at least.'

John Willie stared despondently at the floor. 'By gum, my radio. I'll miss that I shall, it was my best pal. You get to rely on things like that when you live alone, especially so in the long winter months when you can't get out so much. All those friendly folk on Radio Manchester, good plays and discussions.'

There was a strained silence; Irene and David looked at each other sadly. 'Well er...perhaps it's around somewhere,' David began awkwardly, 'after all, we could have missed it, it might have been kicked under...' He stopped quickly.

John Willie stood up. 'Well then, I don't suppose it'll be much use if it's been kicked under something will it? Come on, are we going then?'

As they left the ward, Marion squeezed his arm.

'Cheer up,' she said quietly, 'things could be worse you know. I'll pop round and see you.'

The policeman checked through his list once more, then tucked his notebook back into his pocket.

'Right Mr Greaves, that's it as far as you can tell; radio, toaster, electric fire and some sports shirts. Oh, and of course the gas and electric meters. Usual pattern, all easily disposable items at the second-hand shops, we'll do the rounds of course, the owners of these shops are very co-operative and give us the nod if there's anything comes in that looks a bit shady.'

'Do you think there's much chance of getting this stuff back,' asked John Willie, 'or of catching the thieves?'

The policeman sucked in his breath and spread his hands palms upwards.

'Well, it all depends on whether we get the breaks or not. There have been several of this type of break-in round here recently, all to the same pattern, so if we can make a breakthrough, find out where the stuff is being disposed of for instance, then you might get something back. To be honest though, I wouldn't hold out much hope, these thieves could be from anywhere,

anywhere at all, and just working this patch for a spell. Besides, we're under strength as well, up to our eyes in it.' He stood up and headed for the door. 'We'll let you know if there are any developments,' then he was gone.

Irene and David came through from the kitchen and began to put on their coats. His daughter came up to him and kissed him on the cheek.

'Well dad, we'll have to be getting back to Lytham, Mrs Briggs will see the children off to bed but we told her we wouldn't be late. Of course, we never expected this to have happened when we set off this morning.'

'Right lass, that's alright. Thanks for coming anyway, you too David, I appreciate it very much.'

David cleared his throat. 'Hrrm...er, yes, we'll have to be going now. Sure you'll be alright?'

'Oh aye,' replied John Willie, his eyes straying to the sideboard, 'I'll take my time and get sorted out bit by bit. Oh, our Joan phoned me up in the hospital, she said they'd come over for the day on Saturday.'

Irene's face took on a sour expression. 'Oh yes, and where was she today then? Hazel Grove's a lot nearer than Lytham. She's all talk is that madam, and...' David took her arm. 'Never mind that now love, we'd better get going. Right dad, we'll be over at weekend with the kids. See you then.'

Ater he'd waved them off in their car, John Willie went back in and picked up the photograph of Florrie from the sideboard, and stared at it thoughtfully. The glass was broken and splintered; they'd found it on the floor, it seemed as though it had been trodden on. He sat down in his armchair and spread a newspaper on his knee, then began to remove the broken glass, lovingly and tenderly.

He felt bad, bitter and disappointed. Disappointed in mankind; it seemed as though the world was turning rotten. Ransacking of ordinary terraced houses was commonplace these days, poor people were more often the victims of thieves than rich people. The ones with a bit of brass could afford to pay for burglar alarms, special locks and suchlike things. The ordinary folk might not have a house full of jewels, gold and silver plate and that sort of thing, but there was always the gas and electric meters wasn't there? Little radios, record players, easily disposable items the policeman said. My God, what's the world coming to?

He stood up, and replaced the photograph on the sideboard. 'I'll get a new piece of glass for that,' he said half to himself, then looking closely at the picture of the woman with the kindly face, dark brown wavy hair, and intelligent, loving eyes, he murmured, 'I'm almost glad you're not here to see this mess love.'

A rat-tat-tat on his front door knocker brought

him back down to earth, and he thought it a bit late for callers at his house. When he opened the front door he was surprised to see Marion, the cheery nurse standing there, a great big smile on her jolly face. 'Hello dad,' she said, 'well, are you going to let me in or are you afraid of what the neighbours might say?'

'Oh…er, hello love, no, come in.'

When they were inside she handed him the parcel she had brought with her. '(Here, a little present for you.'

John Willie looked at her, taken aback. 'A present, for me?'

'Yes you daft ha'p'orth, for you. Well go on, open it.'

Stripping off the wrappings he found inside a brand new transistor radio. He stared at it for a few seconds, unable to speak. 'Well,' he began, swallowing the lump in his throat, 'I don't know, I just don't know what to say.'

'Then say nowt,' she said, 'we had a whip round in the wards, didn't take long to get enough for that. Anyway I'm off now so you can have a good listen. I'll be round again in a day or two to see if it's working alright.'

As he watched Marion stride off down the street, John Willie couldn't help feeling he'd been a bit hasty earlier on with his judgement; the world wasn't such a bad place after all, there were still plenty of damn good folk knocking about.

It's My Life Isn't It?

Nell Harwood

She was fifteen, it was 1951, and today she had left school. Her form mistress Miss Forbes had pleaded with her to reconsider.

'You are much too bright to waste your talents in a cotton mill, you have a good brain, use it! Stay on to the sixth form,' she urged.

Jane did not comprehend, she wasn't listening, her mind was closed, filled with thoughts of the money she would have, of being able to buy nice clothes, use make-up, she would be independent. She wanted to forget school, she wasn't a child anymore, Miss Forbes didn't seem to realise, she was an adult.

She didn't feel very adult that first day at the mill, she had presented herself alone at the office as requested, her Mother was so angry with her because of her insistence on leaving school, she had refused to accompany Jane. She was met by the weaving manager, a Mr Kay, a kindly looking man in his fifties, he was wearing dark thick trousers and a dark cotton jacket. She couldn't help thinking as he introduced himself, that he had a kind of greyish look about him, his clothes, his face, his hair seemed dull somehow, without contrast, he looked...she searched for the word, he looked dusty, yes that's it Jane thought, dusty, how peculiar. Before she could surmise further Mr Kay opened a large door and as she followed, she was shocked to a standstill by a hell of a noise. It was deafening, a continuous assault on her eardrums, her mind went numb, her ears were bursting at the explosion of noise that bombarded them, she was, for several moments completely disorientated. She wanted to run, to get away from that remorseless clamour and din.

Mr Kay put a reassuring hand on the bemused girl's arm as they moved on, past the rows of clattering looms, tended mostly by women and girls, wearing bright overalls. She stared around, the first stupifying shock lessening as her ears became more accustomed to the rhythm of the noise. She knew now why Mr Kay looked dusty, the greyish dust was everywhere, it clung to the looms forming clumps of fluff, and it hung in the air like a cloud. Half way down the shed they stopped, the manager beckoned over a plump middle aged lady and spoke to her. Jane looked on in amazement, how could they make themselves heard above the unending clatter of machines and whirring shuttles. She realised when the woman looked at her and spoke, that they didn't communicate by sound, but by lip-reading, looking directly into her face the woman mouthed, 'I am going to teach you how to weave.' Jane was surprised at herself, she had understood, she had been able to *see* what the woman had said.

Months passed, she could hardly believe it but she had actually got used to the endless din. Jessie her instructor had been patient and kind, she had worked as a weaver for over twenty five years and had passed on her skill and experience to Jane. She had used gestures and mouthed instructions so that after only a few weeks Jane had felt confident enough to tend her own looms, and what's more, could lip-read now with the best of them.

She never asked herself in those early years if she was satisfied with her lot, she took her life for granted, there was a camaraderie in the mill amongst the women and girls. If a weaver had a shuttle trap, which meant that the shuttle had stopped in the middle and had broken many of the warp threads, the weavers working each side would run the other looms for her, leaving the unlucky weaver free to spend the next hour drawing the broken ends on the idle loom. A loom not working meant less money on pay day. They would giggle as they dodged the overlooker's ever watchful eye, to sneak into the toilets for a quick smoke. He always looked suspiciously at a girl as she came back to her looms deliberately taking out his watch from the top pocket of his waistcoat, he would look at it, and then look at the girl, shaking his head reproachfully, she would laugh, but all the same she knew she had better stay by her looms for the rest of the morning, it wouldn't be wise to let him catch her a second time. The talk and gossip was of boys and husbands, of dancing on a Saturday night at the Savoy to Tommy Smith's Band, of sitting on the back row at the pictures, and being shocked by stories of the lads who went too far, the ones who tried to put a hand up a girl's skirt. They educated each other about sex, about living their lives according to the moral code of the time. If their world was limited, their lives shallow, they were not aware, and were mostly content, they never question-ed, never thought their world could be different.

Jane was twenty three when she first had thoughts about wanting her life to change. At a wedding of an old school friend, she met up again with Betty. Betty and she had been bosom friends at school. They had shared everything in the intense way that thirteen and fourteen year olds often do. They read romantic poetry, they talked incessantly about life with a capital 'L'. After Jane left school they had lost touch Betty had opted to stay on and take 'O' and 'A' levels.

Jane had become engrossed in the world of work, and the few times they had met they had seemed miles apart. Jane hadn't wanted to hear about school, she had put all that behind her, Betty simply couldn't visualise what working in a weaving shed was all about, and so their meetings grew fewer as both girls became absorbed in their own lives, they drifted apart, with nothing in common anymore.

They greeted each other with genuine pleasure. Betty looked poised and confident, she was well dressed and when she spoke her voice did not have the pronounced Oldham accent.

'You've changed,' Jane said, a tinge of envy in her tone. 'What have you being doing all these years?' Betty told her about her life to date, about how she had got her 'A' levels and had gone to university, and obtained her degree.

'I couldn't decide what I wanted to do at first,' she chatted on, 'I had several offers, I finally plumped for the firm I work for now, they buy and sell all over the world, I've been abroad a few times, it's a super job, I meet lots of interesting people, and the pay is pretty good too. What about you, what have you been up to all these years?' she enquired with interest.

'Oh,' Jane said, trying to keep her voice light. 'I'm fine, you know me, I've got everything I ever wanted.' She started to gabble on then about the bride, the people they knew, anything to ward off Betty's questions. She couldn't bring herself to tell her old friend that she was still doing the same things today, that she'd been doing at sixteen.

At home that night she had a lot to think about.

'I wish I had a job like hers,' she sighed

enviously. 'She is lucky,' and then being honest with herself knew that it wasn't luck. Betty had earned what she had attained. Betty hadn't thought she knew best, she had listened to advice. Jane thought back, and could hear again Miss Forbes pleading with her. Her parents too, they had tried so hard to convince her that she must stay on at school, they had so wanted her to take advantage of the opportunities denied to them. But no, of course she knew best what she wanted, it was her life she had screamed at them defiantly, and they had eventually given in and let her have her way. What a fool I've been she told herself, I was cleverer than Betty too, she reflected, if only I'd listened, who knows what I could have become. If only, but now it was too late, she had missed her chance, she had thrown it away for the lure of easy money. She had wanted to be independent. Well, she was wasn't she? Jane wept. She moped around for several days feeling very sorry for herself. She just couldn't go on, she thought rather dramatically, but what alternative did she have? She groaned aloud as she pictured her future, running four looms for the rest of her life, going on, like Jessie, for thirty years, filling shuttles and watching those looms clatter back and forth. Thirty more years. She thought again of the smart confident Betty, the catalyst of her discontent. No, no, she thought hopelessly, not another thirty years.

As if by coincidence, Jane saw a notice in the local Chronicle that same week. Miss Forbes her old teacher was retiring, and the school was inviting any of her old pupils to attend her farewell evening if they so wished. Jane decided to go.

Miss Forbes had hardly changed over the years. As they shook hands the teacher said, 'Ah yes, Jane, one of my brighter girls, but one of my foolish ones if I remember correctly,' she added.

Impulsively Jane said, 'May I visit you?'

Miss Forbes looked keenly at her for a moment and then 'Of course. What about next week, I'm going to have lots of time on my hands from now on, visitors will be most welcome, will Tuesday evening suit you, eight o'clock?'

She greeted Jane warmly that first evening. As she ushered her into the living room she chatted, trying to put the girl at her ease, giving her time, waiting until Jane was ready to talk. Over coffee, she questioned her visitor gently, about her parents, her boyfriends, casual inconsequential pleasantries that helped her guest to relax, and she watched and waited.

Suddenly the dam burst, Jane began to talk, the words flooded from her as she told Miss Forbes about seeing Betty, about how dissatisfied she had become since that time, about how hopeless her life seemed to be, how she regretted wasting her chances, and she ended despairingly, 'It is too late now isn't it? I'm twenty three, I'm too old.'

Miss Forbes smiled wryly and said, 'Twenty three. Yes, it's quite an age to be.' She took Jane's hand as she continued, 'Believe me, even to be twenty three, doesn't mean it's too late.'

The gentle irony was lost on Jane as the questions tumbled forth, 'Can you help me? What must I do?' her voice eager and excited.

That evening with Miss Forbes was the first of many. She advised Jane to go to night school, and with her old teacher's help she found that she could discipline herself to study, to reading, to learning. Her natural talent and aptitude developed, and for the first time since leaving school, Jane was really using her brain. She had never worked harder and she had never been happier. She visited Miss Forbes every week, and in spite of the age difference the relationship developed from that of teacher and pupil, into a deep and lasting friendship. Jane knew that without her friend's encouragement she would have given up long ago.

The mill now was just a place to earn a living while she studied, she had passed five 'O' levels and was working hard for her 'A's, and so she hadn't really taken a lot of notice when her workmates discussed rumours about the mill not getting the orders. There had been rumours before, but the mill had kept going. In a place like this there were always rumours going around about something or other. This time though it wasn't a rumour, this time notices had been posted, telling workers that due to lack of orders, the mill owners regretted that they had no choice, but to close down the mill. In six months time all workers would be redundant. For the last few years the textile industry had been in difficulties. Almost every week Jane had read in the newspapers about some mill somewhere going on short time or another closing down, but it couldn't happen to their mill, or so she had thought, their mill had not closed down during the really bad times in the twenties and thirties. Well that's what everyone said.

On that last day, before the looms stopped clattering for ever, and the giant steam engine in the basement turned for the last time, the weavers had a footings. They brought sandwiches, cream cakes and beer, and one group even brought champagne. Although the engine was still turning the looms were silent, as the weavers sang and told jokes and screamed with laughter that had a touch of hysteria. As they prepared to leave on that last afternoon, most of the older weavers were crying openly, for many, forty years of their lives had been spent in this shed, it was for them saying goodbye to a known past, and for the first time having to cope with an uncertain future. For the young, change was a challenge, for the older women, the change was being forced upon them, and they were devastated.

Jane at twenty five felt a sadness that surprised her, in spite of her desire to get away that had obsessed her for almost three years, now the moment had arrived, she couldn't help thinking of the friends she would probably never see again, of the good times, and suddenly she realised that she was glad that she had had the experience, that whatever the future might hold, her years here in the weaving shed hadn't been wasted years after all, they had helped to shape and form the person she had become.

Everything and everyone changed with time. Oldham the town she lived in would be different as more mills closed. As she progressed with her education and looked for new opportunities, who could tell what life would have in store for her. Maybe she would be a career woman holding down a responsible job, or perhaps she would marry and have children and be able to pass on to them the benefits of her education, and, she wondered, if I ever have a daughter who at sixteen wants to go her own way, what will I advise? Will I allow her to make her own mistakes? I wonder.

Trafford Park — a poem of love and hate

Ken Craven

By scrapyard railway wagons
now disused, lie the lovers,
caressing each breath
that takes these treasured moments
down the canal
where Guinness boats
are sleeping in their magnificence.

A seagull flies
above the football ground
whose lighted arms stretch out
to grasp the sulphured smoke
thrown out by
generations of generators,
sending power to the hives
where bees are making money
and machines
to drive along
this dank inferno.

A road, too long
too narrow
once twisted between
a garden,
long since changed
to a cemetery of grey
where trees are built
of brick and steel
and the fruits they bear
are chemicals of death
creating a market
for sheet-metal coffins.
Lake of laughter
where are you now?

Nazi bombers missed us then
but next time...
next time
I'll be there
shining my torch
searching
for a flower.

Leaving

Heather Leach

It was a June day, warm from the early morning, fresh and tempting. She had opened the front door and was gazing outwards and upwards into the sky. Her back was a dark broad shape blocking the light, the sun spilling around her into the hallway. I couldn't see her face, but I knew something was wrong and I was afraid. She stood so quietly, turned away from us, almost a stranger, and we waited, watchful and uneasy. After what seemed a long time, she turned, smiling, bringing the light back with her.

'I know, let's go on a picnic,' she said, 'I'll see what we've got to eat in the pantry. Come on Barbara, you can go and buy some lemonade, and the little ones can butter the bread.' She was back with us, our mother, calm and reassuring. I breathed again and taking the money she gave me, I ran out into the day.

We lived in Newall Green, in Wythenshawe, and in the early 1950's it was all new. The pavement, the street was white, chalky white, glaring in the sun. The houses were made of sharp red bricks that scraped your hands on the corners. Our road was on the edge of the country. I thought then that this country was very close to the wilderness, that the fields at the back of us stretched for miles and miles and that after the fields came — what? I didn't know. Some free, open region with no fences or hedges, the beginning of the jungle perhaps, or the desert, that's what I thought then, when I was a child. Now I know that this green place where we walked and played and went for picnics was just a narrow strip between our council estate and the surburban villages of Cheshire. Two or three farms wide, this threatened borderland, was my wild playground.

We walked slowly along the lane, mother pushing the big old pram with my two sisters in it, and me walking alongside. There was a large bag stuffed into the bottom of the pram, I knew this wasn't the picnic food because that was behind the pillow.

'What's that bag for mum?' There was no answer. I looked up at her, squinting to see her face. She was staring straight ahead, her eyes were red. Was she crying? I looked away, embarrassed and disturbed.

The way to the picnic field was down Clay Lane, a winding journey through trees and bramble bushes, skirting round Baguley chest hospital, past the new factory. These were old lanes, shaped by old times and old ways, a farmer still carried his milk in a horse drawn cart, the cows drank at a deep clear pool, shaded by alders. I drove down there recently, to see how it had changed, to see if I could catch a taste of those summer days. The lanes are still there, the green belt, buffering the smug wealth of Prestbury and Hale, but everything else has changed. The hedges are thinner, poorer and the trees look small and weak. I drove around and around, and found only my own perspective. Locked inside my moving window, I was a visitor, a tourist, snooping on the past.

When we arrived at the place, mother spread out the cloth, we arranged the sandwiches and biscuits, and put the lemonade bottle under the hawthorn, Mum said it was too early to eat anything yet and to go and play. The two little ones rolled off, pulling at the grass and waving their legs in the air. I stayed close by my mother, afraid to go far. Usually, on days like this, she smelled the air, and made us take deep breaths. 'Get some oxygen into your lungs' she would say. She liked to tell us the name of plants and flowers, told to her by her father who had come from a farm in the Mourne mountains. She loved the slow laziness of these afternoons, the smallness, the sweet dependence of her children. She loved these new summer days, the rich grass, the buzzing stillness, just as she loved the dark winter, the fire, the tea by the hearth. When my own children were babies, and I was complaining to her about the work and the restrictions, she warned me not to go too fast. 'Those times when they're little, when they need you so much, those are the best times,' she said, but I was impatient and different from her. If she had any other ambition, than to be our mother, I never knew it, and just as she loved life in all its particularities, so I loved her, like a flower loves the sun.

This day she was withdrawn, lying back on the grass and closing her eyes. I lay down too, beside her, stretching out my arms from my body and digging my fingers into the roots of the field. I felt the world tilt underneath me, tipping me backwards, forwards into the deep sky. I jumped up, unable to be still any longer, and ran to the end of the field. Here below the hedge was a dry streambed where you could crawl along between the ancient bushes and make a den in a dusty hollow. I drew dolls and monsters in the sand with a stick, and made them talk to each other, muttering and whispering under my breath. I forgot all about my mother, lying inexplicably silent on the green earth.

I began to creep around the edge of the field, behind the branches, secret and stealthy. I meant to come near to my sisters before they knew I was there and to leap out like a tiger, fierce and frightening. I stepped on something, and pulled back peering down at it, a vague object in the dappled light. There was a dark eye looking at me and a claw, yellow, wrinkled. I held my breath, paralysed, transfixed with horror. It was a dead crow, lying on its back in this hidden place, one black wing spread out on the ground, the other folded tight into its side. It stared blindly at me, its cruel dead beak sharp and dangerous. There were no obvious wounds, but I could smell blood and flies and the body looked misshapen and wrong. I scrambled backwards through the branches, falling out into the light, and running then, running towards her, towards safety and my mother.

She had taken the big bag out of the pram, and was rummaging in it, sorting out the things inside. As I came up to her, gasping and breathless, she tried to put it away, to hide what she was doing. But I could see the clothes, her spare skirt and cardigan, and there too, were my pyjamas and my sister's nightdress. I looked at her. Were we going to sleep somewhere else? Where were we going? Where would my bed be? I could not speak, but I could see from my mother's face that she could hear my voice. I started to cry.

Every night after I had gone to bed, I heard them talking. Sitting at the top of the stairs and listening, I could never quite catch what they said. My father's voice was deep and loud, but his words were blurred and empty of meaning. One night my Grandmother came out of her room and made me get back in next to my sister.

'Don't worry,' she said, 'it's me they're arguing about.' I fell asleep to the droning sound of the voices downstairs. In the evening and in the night, when my father was at home there were shadows in the house, there was no peace or laughter, and I was filled with a restless anxiety. Only when the morning came, and he had gone to work did my mother relax, putting the kettle on, opening the windows, letting in the day.

She didn't let me cry for long. 'Come on Barbara, don't be a baby, you're my big girl, let's get this food ready, you go and bring the lemonade.' We ate our picnic as the sun shone down, hotter and hotter. The food tasted of grass and flowers, and the lemonade drunk out of the bottle made us cough and splutter. There was nobody else about, just the four of us, just my mother and her three daughters, a woman and her children, together in a quiet field, at the edge of the city.

We walked slowly down the lane beside the farm. The cows were standing by the fence ready for milking, waiting for the farmer to let them into the shed. We stood on the gate and stroked their backs and they twitched their skin and stared at us sideways with nervous eyes. I picked dandelion clocks and blew the time away. She had pushed the bag right under the pram cover, and now she began walking faster, so that I nearly had to run to keep up.

'Right, time you lot had some exercise, one, two, one, two, hup, two, one, two.' We marched along, me swinging my arms, like a soldier, her singing and beating time on the pram handle. Then I stopped.

'Mum, where are we going? Where are we going to?' She looked down at me, her face dark for a moment, hiding the sun. Then smiled, reassuring.

'We're going home, it's getting late, it's time for your dad's tea.' Of course we were going home. Where else? Where else was there for her to go? I started marching again, and she sang for me all the way back to our own front door.

Where The Heart Is

Alrene Hughes

Erin snuggled down between the crisp linen sheets enjoying the comfort and security they brought her in this strange room, smelling as they did of sea breezes and the soft air of home. Outside the uncurtained window heavy rain fell relentlessly on the grey tiled roofs that stretched row after boring row all the way from Newton Heath to Miles Platting. The street lamps cast an orange glow over the room and by their light she could just make out the head of Deirdre her sister and the child's arm cradling a 'Tiny Tears' doll — ample compensation to a seven year old for loss of home and country.

In the next room Erin could hear her Mother and Father laying the carpet and shifting furniture. Earlier her Father using giant scissors had struggled until his fingers blistered to cut the old carpet to the shape of the new room. She pictured her Father and Mother down on their knees, each holding a brick wrapped in a rag, pounding, smoothing, persuading the carpet into the corners of the room.

'It's no good, John, it'll never look right and the furniture looks so shabby now I see it in this strange place.'

'Oh it'll be alright, Mary, don't fret.'

But Erin, as she drifted off to sleep, caught the sound of a sob with each thud of the brick.

Her first full day in England dawned dull and grey and a steady drizzle fell from a murky sky: maybe it was true what they said about Manchester. Soon the whole family were dressed and ready for their first trip into the city that was now their home. They caught the bus on the busy Oldham Road and Deirdre and Erin rushed ahead upstairs to the front seats where they would get the best view. There was no one else on the top deck and the conductor was clearly annoyed at having to climb the stairs and walk the length of the bus to collect their fares.

'Two and two halves to Manchester, please,' said her father.

'What d'ya mean Manchester? You're in Manchester. It's all Manchester as far as the eye can see.'

'I meant the city centre. We want to go to the centre of Manchester.'

'You mean Piccadilly?'

'Yes, I mean Piccadilly. Will you give us a shout when we get there?'

'Oh you'll know when you get there without me telling you,' said the conductor as he handed over the tickets and change and then he marched off muttering to himself about someone called Paddy.

From the top deck of the bus Erin could see

the city stretching away in the distance in every direction. She tried to take in the strange land-scape of factories, high rise flats and those never ending rows of 'Coronation Streets'. But there was something about the lay of the land that made Erin feel uncomfortable, disorientated. She had no idea whether they were travelling North, South, East or West and it was a while before she realised why — there was neither sea nor mountain by which she could get her bearings.

In Belfast she always knew in which direction she was travelling. She had only to lift her eyes to seek out the Cave Hill and the Black Moun-tain or the long ribbon of the lough to know where she was in relation to the rest of the world. Erin closed her eyes for a moment and imagined herself again on the Cave Hill, breathing clean crisp air and looking down on Belfast spread out below her, its huge shipyard gantries like pieces of a child's Meccano set in the distance. The city always looked so peaceful cradled in the hills but it was like the stage of a Roman amphitheatre where noise like a bomb blast in the night carried to every ear the warn-ing 'You are not safe. You are not safe.'

She opened her eyes suddenly and looked again at the unfamiliar landscape. Here was a city so vast she couldn't see the end of it, but it was a place, so she'd heard, that was peaceful, welcoming and free of prejudice.

Piccadilly was bustling, full of people in a hurry, flowing like a river around Erin and her family as they stood looking up at the buildings that gave the city its character. They saw the Hotel Piccadilly with its broad top balanced precariously on a narrow base and wondered how would-be guests ever found their way into it. The Eagle Star building with its blue/green roof turned up into points like a star-shaped saucer had them gazing upwards and pointing. But it was Lewis's department store which finally drew them like a magnet off the busy street and through the doors which blew warm air in their faces — a portend of the luxury to be found within.

The food hall was vast; nothing but things to eat as far as the eye could see: whole counters just full of cheese, another with cream cakes and gateaux big enough to satisfy the giant Finn McCool and everywhere busy hurrying people who seemed to take this epicurean spectacle in their stride.

Slowly, like tourists taking in the sights of an exotic land, the family journeyed through the shop, upwards and upwards, floor after floor, until, in time for lunch, they came to a restaurant large enough to do justice to the vast emporium below.

At the door Erin hesitated, struck by the waves of smell and sound; steak and kidney pie, babbling voices, and the scrape of a hundred ill-mannered knives upon plates.

'Come on, Erin. I want my dinner.' Deirdre pulled her sister towards the self-service counter which wound like a ribbon along one wall. They joined the queue of people pushing wooden trays that looked like carriages on a train stopping every so often to be loaded with food.

'I'm having chips,' said Deirdre 'with tomato sauce all over the top.' The woman in front of them, all tweed, twinset and pearls stared down at the child who swung from the shelf where the trays rested and something in her look reminded Erin of her mother's face when the tinkers called at their Belfast home trying to sell dishcloths and to read palms as though they were real Romanies and not itinerants from Donegal.

Behind little glass doors, each with a handle and a green sign saying 'Lift' Erin could see huge plates of salad.

'Mammy,' she whispered, wary of looking unsophisticated, or worse, ill-mannered, 'just look at that funny pie. It has hard-boiled egg in the middle.'

'Well have it if you want it, dear. Sure you'll have to be trying these things now.' Erin took the Gala pie salad from the glass case and wondered in an absent-minded sort of way, how they got the egg in the middle. Then a large bosomed woman in a check overall and a tiny hat over a shock of ginger hair leaned over the counter and said loudly 'Do you want spring onions on that, luv?' Erin didn't answer; she hadn't quite caught what the woman had said; it took a bit of getting used to this Mancunian accent.

'Have them anyway, luv. It's all included in the price,' and she dropped two shiny white onions from her tongs onto the plate of salad. Erin looked down at them in amazement so, too, did her Mother and Father. Then they looked at each other and began to laugh.

'They're scallions,' said Mammy smiling in disbelief, 'They eat the wrong end of scallions in England!'

To complete her strange meal Erin chose a cake like a slab of custard between flaky pastry with icing on the top and followed the rest of her family to the check-out.

'That'll be two pounds, fifteen shillings and ninepence,' said the cashier perched on a high stool and Erin's father handed over three pound notes.

''Ere what's this? Monopoly money?' she held the Ulster pound notes up to the light.

'No, it's Ulster money — it's legal tender,' he said. Erin felt a glow of embarrassment surround them as the cashier called out to a woman shovelling chips onto a plate.

''Ere, Elsie, ever seen one of these before?' But Elsie gave Ulster Bank the thumbs down.

'It's that there foreign currency,' she said with all the solemnity of a judge passing a life sentence, 'it'll not do here.'

Her father had no defence and for one awful moment Erin thought they would have to put all the food back, but her mother saved the day by producing from her purse a five pound note as English as...spring onions.

As Erin settled down to eat her lunch she wondered about the sort of people who squeezed hard-boiled eggs into pork pies, ate the wrong end of scallions, sandwiched cold custard between flaky pastry and didn't know good money when they saw it.

Later that evening in the flat they sat around the coal fire Daddy had lit after he had discovered bags of coal for sale in a corner shop called, for some obscure reason, an 'outdoor'.

'These bags'll do rightly 'til we find a proper coal man — one that delivers through bombs and bullets' he added and they all laughed at that, thinking of Uncle Frank, a coalman back home, whose proudest boast to his Ardoyne customers was 'Brown's coal beats bombs and bullets.'

They left the light off, preferring the gentle glow of the fire. Faded, heavy curtains shut out the night and the room, so strange before, was beginning to feel more comfortable, as though the furniture had eased itself into place.

'Can we have a sing-song, Daddy, like we do at home?' pleaded Deirdre.

'This is home now,' said Erin.

'You know what I mean,' said the child, a

peeved look on her face, 'like proper home.' Erin caught her Mother's eye and saw a look of uneasiness flash across her face. But Daddy had already lifted the guitar from where it rested in the chimney corner and had begun to tune it up.

'Alright, Deirdre, what'll it be?' he said, already strumming the chords of 'Belle of Belfast City'. Deirdre always asked for the same song. It was one she sang while skipping and she liked to sing the verse and have them all join in on the chorus.

Next her mother sang 'Carrickfergus'. Its haunting tune always made Erin feel sad but it was such a beautiful song and suited her mother's voice so well that she never minded the sadness for the pleasure it gave her. After that they ran through a dozen different songs and with each their spirits soared. As Erin looked around the cosy room and saw the faces of her family flushed with the warmth of the fire and the pleasure of singing, she felt, at last, happy and safe.

Outside a stiff wind had blown the rainclouds away. It would be a better day tomorrow.

Where We Live

Kathleen Bohannon

Picture if you will
A city on a hill,
That's not where we live.

Picture if you will
A meadow full of larks,
A stream that flows on by,
A haunting curlew's cry,
That's not where we live.

Picture if you will
The dark satanic mills,
Whose shadows linger still.
Where people poor and cold,
Much too soon grow old,
And much too young
Just die.
That's where we live.

Home For Whitsun

Elsie Maskell

The old Dutch clock on the parlour mantelshelf struck seven o'clock, the chimes woke Sally Dawson.

She looked sleepily around the small bedroom which she occupied in the terraced house, belonging to her aunt.

Before she had left home ten years ago, Sally had shared this little room with her cousin Lily. Smiling to herself she thought of all the stuff both of them had crammed into the small old-fashioned wardrobe, her aunt Ellen had always been very house proud, and Sally could still remember being constantly reminded to 'keep your room tidy you pair', and she had thought, 'no chance, we need a bigger bedroom'.

'Breakfast's ready!' her aunt shouted from the bottom of the stairs.

'Be down in a jiffy', was the reply.

Sausage, egg and beans for breakfast went down very well, that was another thing that hadn't changed, food was a ritual up here, especially Sunday dinner.

While Sally was eating her meal, she glanced through the kitchen window, Mrs Kavanagh was hanging her washing out, that was another tradition in Manchester, weekly routine, every day was used for different domestic tasks.

'I think we'll go on Market Street, have a look round, then go down to George Barker's, I want a few more cheques from him, Molly Dillon and Bridie Jordon haven't got frocks for their little lasses yet, and it's Whit Sunday this Sunday.'

What a great deal of sacrifice went into dressing the children for this great local event, each mother wanting her child to be star of her church's part of the procession.

These events were as much a part of Manchester and Salford's life and culture, as were The Hallé, the day's outing to Blackpool for the poor children, and the charabanc trips, not forgetting the Saturday matinée at the Empire Cinema. They were the heartbeat of the people of Manchester.

Walking to the bus stop, Sally and Aunt Ellen stopped to talk to at least six people — this was one of the many things Sally missed — the friendly people of Manchester, back in Stratford-upon-Avon the people were not very homely. Eventually they reached town, one or two items were bought and some groceries and fruit from the barrows. Making their way back to the bus station they boarded a bus for Cross Lane and Regent Road.

As they turned into Broad Street, Sally noticed that Hankinson Street, or 'Hanky Park' as it was affectionately known was being rebuilt and high rise flats were taking shape. Sally had known quite a few people who had lived in the place where Walter Greenwood author of the famous story, 'Love On The Dole' once lived. Bringing her thoughts back to this moment in time, Sally noticed a large vacant plot, where there used to be several shops. There had been three bespoke tailors and a couple of grocery stores, one of which belonged to Mr and Mrs Brindle. They sold everything that was saleable, from greengrocery down to hairpins, and odd pieces of furniture which were sold almost before they were unloaded from the battered little van.

And now it was all gone. Sally wondered what would be built in their place when she visited Manchester again.

They reached Barker's drapery shop. Being so close to Whitsun, there was quite a bit of trade going on, last minute buying of socks and shoes, ribbons and bows, all in aid of the big event.

Aunt Ellen went over to the counter, 'Hello George, how are you? How's the family?'

'Fine thanks, are you and Joe well? I see you have Sally with you.'

'Yes,' Ellen replied, 'she has been up for the week, she's going back on Monday.'

'I'll go and get your cheques, twenty wasn't it?' He appeared a minute or two later and handed over the twenty cheques, 'See you next week then!' Ellen nodded. After a final glance around the glass cases in the shop they left.

Walking down Ordsall Lane, they met one or two old neighbours coming out of the corner shop, one of the women seemed a little tipsy, due to the fact that ale was sold in the Off Licence. Sally realised they had both had a few glasses while buying their groceries.

As they reached Hawarth's Mill, standing silent and empty, there was a sadness that overcame Sally. She felt as though part of her life was closely entwined in this big grim building, as indeed it was. This was where she had worked when she had left school, and she had stayed there until she left Manchester. What memories came flooding back — the sound of clogs on the cobblestones, the clatter of the looms in the weaving shed. The old mill seemed to come alive with the sounds of yesterday. Sally thought of the friends she had known, where were they now? One memory stood out above the others — that of the 'Cotton Queen' event, one of the most important yearly occasions in the Lancashire calendar. The lucky girl chosen to be Cotton Queen for a year was the one judged to be the prettiest mill girl in Lancashire. Once she was chosen, a glittering ball was held in Blackpool, where she was duly crowned, what excitement and what a wonderful night everyone had. Oh yes, those memories would always remain a part of Sally's life, no matter where she was.

On reaching home, Sally said, 'Do you want me

to get tea auntie?'

'Yes love, if you will, Joe will be home soon,
I will go up Cheetham Street to the butchers, and
then to the greengrocers, I won't be long.'

As Sally prepared the meal she realised she had
almost forgotten the Free Trade Hall that evening. She had booked seats for a friend and herself
to hear the Hallé, as she always managed one
performance whenever she came home, nothing
to beat the Hallé, thought Sally.

Saturday was relatively quiet and the weekend
shopping was done. Normally a lot of the popula-
tion would have been going to the football
match, whichever team was playing at home,
either City or United, but this Saturday there
wasn't one — a most unusual occurrence. Sally
helped her aunt with the housework, washed
her hair, and then went to Bridie Jordan's to see
if she could help her get her six children ready
for the big day tomorrow.

Now Saturday night by any standard was
drama night for the children, the reason being
the ritual of bath night and more so this particular night. First of all, the big copper was filled with water, and a fire was lit underneath it.
When the water was hot enough the large tin
bath was brought out, cold water poured in,
followed by the right amount of hot water, then
the children were called in from play. This didn't
always meet with the children's approval
especially if they were in the middle of play,

however, anyone who didn't conform knew what to expect.

The first act was the hair washing, with a kind of soap called 'Soft', this was poured onto the head, Mother then proceeded to rub and tug, finally screwing the hair into a bunch nearly lifting the poor little victim off the floor. The hair and head was then thoroughly dried which was most painful for the child concerned.

Next step in the ritual was into the bath, where the unfortunate child was soaped and scrubbed, ears poked, and special attention paid to the neck. All this amid cries of 'Oh, Aagh,' and then the final indignity — a large jug of warm water was poured over head and body with gasps for breath and splutterings. When it was all over they emerged, pink little bodies and faces and hair that stuck out like hedgehog needles.

Each child followed the same routine, some enjoyed it more than others. The final act of the drama was hair curling. Now this was something! Each little girl sat on a chair while Mam put strips of cloth in to 'make it curly'. By this time the poor little kids were exhausted and could only sit there and take it. Sally smiled when she thought of the times she had gone through the same performance, but never mind, at the end of all this was a nice reward — lovely clean clothes on and a nightdress that looked like a long frock with buttons down the front. Little boys wore what looked like a long nightshirt.

The last thing was a mug of cocoa and a butty, and so to bed.

Whit Sunday dawned fine and warm. Sally felt that old excitement that she had always felt on these occasions. She remembered when she herself had walked with 'St Cyprians' and how proud she had felt, as she had walked behind the minister, the altar boys and the beautiful banner the church possessed. Now she had a family of her own, but came north every year to relive her childhood memories.

Aunt Ellen, Uncle Joe and herself had managed to get a good viewing point at the corner of Market Street, having got there early. They settled down to wait for the first signs of the processions.

The crowds were good humoured, and orderly as always, patiently waiting for the first children to come into view.

After what seemed an age the strains of music came, on the warm summer breeze the sound of drums, people murmured, 'here they come!' as a ripple of excitement spread through the crowds.

The first children emerged into sight to exclamations of 'Oh, aren't they lovely bless them', and 'there's our church there', and 'them little 'uns must be tired', all this to delighted applause.

Looking at these little children dressed in white with their veils and carrying beautiful little bouquets, Sally could not help but think of the sacrifices made to keep this old tradition alive, by people who had little or nothing, but pay they would, no matter what the hardship. And so on this lovely June day, as each church came into its own, Sally knew that wherever she went to live, she would always return for this yearly event.

The last of the processions passed by, bringing in their wake, civic dignitaries, such as the veterans of two world wars, St John's Ambulance, the Women's Voluntary Services and the District Council, to name but a few. As the sounds of the band faded away and the crowds dispersed, the old Cathedral clock chimed out as if in justified contentment. Sally thought what stories these ancient buildings could tell, what sights they had witnessed, standing as guardians in Manchester, for centuries. But now it was all over, and tomorrow she would be going home to a different life, she would miss the old city more than she cared to admit — would miss its people and its life.

Now there was another practice to be carried out before this day was through, and as her aunt opened the front door, several of her neighbours' children trooped in the front gate. This was reward time for them, coins would be given and praise for how nice each one of them looked, but everybody knew how important the pennies were because in a very short time all the finery would be carefully taken off to be replaced with everyday clothes. Strangely enough there was never any opposition to all this carry on. Was it, or could it be because a certain ice cream man called Tuck would be shouting his familiar strain of 'Ice Cream' and large wafers and cornets dripping with raspberry vinegar would be handed out.

Sally stood in the little bedroom. Through the open window she could see the rows of little terraced houses, she wondered how many more would have gone, by the time she visited again. The old city was well in the line of progress.

'Come on Sally! Or you'll miss your train.'

She picked up her suitcase and went downstairs, after a light breakfast Sally said goodbye to her aunt at the front door along with one or two of the neighbours who had come to see her off. She made her way to the bus stop and caught the first bus to Manchester.

The train was already standing at the platform as Sally hurried through the barrier. She boarded the train with only a minute to spare and soon the old familiar London Road Station faded from view.

A New Life in Little Hulton

Joy Openshaw

I well remember the excitement at my terraced home in the middle of Salford when my parents received notice that they were to move to a modern council house in Worsley. We thought that this meant Worsley Village and not Little Hulton as it turned out to be. At that time, thirty five years ago, Little Hulton was part of the Worsley Urban District and that is where the misunderstanding occurred.

Although our two up and two down terraced house was comfortable, we desperately needed better accommodation now that my brothers and I were growing up. Our cramped conditions gave us no privacy.

Our 'front' room with its large window, overlooked the cobbled street. There was no garden and as the neighbours passed by their chatter could be heard as well as the clatter of their clogs on the way to work. We put up net curtains purchased off the Flat Iron Market at Salford to keep prying eyes out of our living room. The big iron fireplace dominated this small room. My mother polished it with black leading until it shone. She made marvellous bread in the oven as everything was warm — ideal for the dough rising in a bowl on the glowing hearth.

In front of the fire was a patterned peg rug made from numerous old coats obtained from local jumble sales. My mother got a piece of sacking and had us cutting up strips of cloth to loop into the sacking with a peg-hook. This made her fingers sore with the rubbing against the rough and coarse sacking. Surrounding the large rug was oil-cloth which was again highly polished and spotless as the rest of the house.

A large wooden table filled the room; its large legs enclosed in 'stockings' made out of old woollies. This was to prevent our dog Rex from sharpening his claws on the table legs. Some historians say that this covering up of table legs was related to the moral values of the Victorians, but in our case it was necessary so that the furniture did not become damaged. A large green baize tablecloth, with bobbles, covered the table top to match the mantelpiece cover over the fireplace.

My mother's best pots were kept on a display cabinet in the corner of the room and were brought out only on the very special occasions such as weddings or funerals.

Our three-piece mock leather suite made the room even more cluttered and dark. This gloomy atmosphere affected our outlook on life.

The back kitchen was no better as the old

cracked slop-stone appeared dirty in spite of all the scouring which it received from my mum. The one tap produced cold water, if we wanted hot water we had to heat it in a big copper pan placed either on the open fire or the antiquated gas stove. The lavatory was down the yard and was frozen up in winter which was most inconvenient!

One Sunday afternoon prior to our departing, we decided to explore our new beginnings. We boarded a bus at Victoria in order to visit the 'promised land' — the site of our new home. We asked the bus conductor to put us off at our destination which turned out to be the Court House at Worsley as that is where we directed him from our description. How happy we were as we viewed the timbered Court House building close to the Bridgewater Canal and Worsley Green.

As we walked over the hump-backed bridge at Worsley Green, we could see that the water in the Bridgewater Canal was rust coloured, but did not know that this was from the iron deposits in the underground canal which drained into The Delph. We sat on the Worsley Green eating our butties and listening to the birds. Occasionally, a highly-coloured pleasure barge would slowly drift by, the crew obviously enjoying themselves on this lazy Sunday afternoon.

My brothers and I chased over Worsley Green clambering up the Monument which was a disused chimney. We jumped down the steps and took photographs of the black and white cottages which surrounded The Green.

We bought a Worsley Guidebook from the village post office and learned that the Bridgewater Canal had been constructed in 1760 to transport coal from the Duke of Bridgewater's mines at Worsley to the thriving city of Manchester which was expanding quickly owing to the Industrial Revolution.

What a historic place this was and weren't we lucky to be going to live there! Uprooting ourselves from the grimy inner city Salford to this pleasant spot didn't seem as traumatic as first envisaged.

So here we all were — mum, dad, me and my three brothers in these idyllic surroundings. Up Worsley Brow we trudged where we could see acres of agricultural land which we thought would be built upon for the Salford overspill estates which had been promised.

In 1947, the Salford City Council, the Lancashire County Council and the Worsley Urban District Council had come together in a tripartite agreement to build the Salford overspill estates for the people who had been displaced from the inner city in the post-war slum clearance programme. What an innovation! This was a forerunner of the New Towns Act and we were the first! What an opportunity to start afresh. We got back home and planned what we would do when we moved into the country.

First of all, my dad made a plan of the house and garden from the outline drawings which the Council had sent us. We decided which furniture would be disposed of and my mother started to think about new curtains, carpets and furniture. But where would the money for all these new things come from? My mother and dad reckoned on spending cash on items such as curtain materials from the market which my mother could run up on the treadle Singer sewing machine left to her by my Gran. Big items such as carpets and furniture would have to be purchased on 'HP' paying so much per week for several years.

A three piece suite was a *must* as was the dining room and bedroom suites. Wouldn't we be posh — just like the scenes on the movies. The house was a hive of activity as we disposed of all our belongings by holding bonfires in the back yard.

What a blow then, when we discovered that it was not Worsley Village we were moving to, but Little Hulton which had been part of the Worsley Urban District Council since the early 1930's.

Little Hulton three miles further north than Worsley towards Farnworth and Bolton, was of a higher elevation and was considered more healthier than Worsley because it got the sea breezes from the Lancashire coast and moorland breezes from Winter Hill. Apparently, we were not the only Salfordians to breath the fresh air of Walkden Moor as it was known, as our ancestors before us had gone there on Sunday School picnics to The Spa at Little Hulton overlooking Winter Hill where there are marvellous sunsets.

As the time for the move approached we were left with some trepidation. Would we fit in? Would we get homesick? What about schools, jobs, shops? We were assured by the Council representative at the numerous meetings held in the local Church hall, that all would be well and everything had been taken into account by the planners.

And so, we packed our few treasures and moved out of Salford. 'Start Afresh' was the motto.

Surprisingly, the move to Little Hulton was well organised. We moved into our three bedroomed council house overlooking a playing field near to the old Roman Catholic Church of St Edmund.

The house was very spacious — three rooms downstairs and three rooms upstairs, with glass doors everywhere. The kitchen and bathroom were fabulous with cream fixtures and fittings. We all set to straight away cleaning thoroughly before the carpet fitters arrived. Fancy us having a fitted carpet — what would our forebears have thought of this luxury? My mother's curtains fitted exactly and now we were ready for the brand new furniture to arrive. We looked out for the furniture van for ages as everyone else on the estate had the same idea. At last it arrived and we could settle down.

As we snuggled into our new beds with crisp new linen sheets it was like being on holiday in a first-class hotel. Strange noises woke us in the morning. Not the clatter of clogs or the hooting of the factory sirens but the chirping of blackbirds, starlings and skylarks. This made us all warm to our new surroundings and the disappointment at not going to live in Worsley Village, was soon forgotten.

We felt at home straight away as all the new streets were named after the area we had just left — Windsor Avenue, Buile Hill Drive, Langworthy Avenue, Trafford Drive, Crescent Drive, Hope Avenue.

As we all came from the same part of Salford we spoke with the same accent. Our Salford accent is different than that of the natives of Little Hulton and Walkden as we clip the ends off our words unlike them with their broad vowels.

Of course, we were bewildered at the beginning with our new environment. At first, we kept to the main roads as we were frightened of getting lost. We knew that the A6 Manchester Road led back into Salford through Walkden and Swinton. We found the shops in these centres but later on huge shopping precincts were built for everyone's benefit which is still continuing today as big firms invest in retailing.

Our gardens were a mess for a couple of years as the land varied from peat to bog, but with fertilisers they soon began to bloom. It is amazing how the gardens have transformed the area over the years. Instead of bleak moorland, the grass is greener and the trees are now mature after thirty years of growth.

My dad moved from the engineering works at Trafford Park to work at a local engineering works already established. We all benefitted as we saw more of him and he did not have bus fares to pay thus leaving us more money. He enjoyed not being stuck at Barton Bridge every morning waiting for the ships to pass along the Manchester Ship Canal.

On Walkden Moor where we now live, was an old school named Blair's after a local benefactress. Her family owned Harison Blair's Chemical Works on Kearsley Moss which is now part of the M61 motorway. The chemicals which have been buried underneath still seep through the earth after all these years — locally known as 'Stink bomb hill'. This chemical infested earth is ideal growing ground for wild orchids which display their colours every year in several secret places only known to the residents of the area.

This old Blair's Sunday School was situated on the other side of the mineral railway line which ran from Mosley Common Colliery to Ashtonfield sidings. Mosley Common Colliery is now closed and prestige houses called 'Ellenbrook Village' are now built there.

To cross the line we had to use wooden bridges which had been in existence long before we arrived. These wooden bridges were so worn that splinters often punctured our fingers. It was a novelty to run across the wooden bridge when the train was approaching. As the steam blew up our clothes and engulfed us, it was like being transported into another world as the sensation was so different.

As the years have passed Blair School became too delapidated to maintain and the land was sold off for bungalows. However, next door is a thriving youth centre with many activities for teenagers such as table tennis, disco dancing, flea markets and community project work.

At first, we returned to our roots in Salford frequently, but as the years have passed we have integrated. Salford inner city has changed. In the place of our terraced houses are multi-storey flats. Private firms are refurbishing the graffiti-ridden dwellings and selling them off to 'yuppies'. At first glance this seems to have improved the area.

Now, Worsley Urban District is part of the City of Salford. Perhaps that was the original intention all those years ago when Salford overspill was first proposed. For us, we have enriched our lives and those of our families.

This is not a dying community, but a *thriving, living one* because of us!

Before Television

John Clare

I can't remember how it all started. Get talking about old times and some folks get carried away.

All I said was 'There's not much to do on Cheetham Hill in the evenings.'

She said 'There used to be...before television.' Then before I could stop her she was off. 'Let's see,' she began 'we had a choice of six picture-houses, we called them the 'flicks', roller skating in Thomas Street, the ice rink in Derby Street or a dance at the Liberal Club. Of course the best dances were at Cheetham Town Hall Assembly Rooms. A real sprung floor, the best in Manchester.'

I thought it best to humour her. 'Six picture-houses' I exclaimed, but her thoughts raced on.

'There was the Globe near Woolworths, the Greenhill and the Shakespeare down Halliwell Lane. Further down the hill was the Temple and then the Riviera just past Queens Road on the left. Oh! I forgot the best one. The Premier near Waterloo Road, they had a cafe upstairs.'

My patience was growing thin, 'But I'm talking about Cheetham Hill, Manchester.'

'The same place young fellow,' she replied but her tone was cold.

It was time for drastic measures. 'But what did

you do after the 'flicks'?' I asked.

She paused but only for a moment. 'There was always Quinns the herbalist. Hot or cold 'Vim-to' or dandelion and burdock but our group always used to go to that Italian cafe. Beautiful ice cream, peanuts, monkey nuts and the rest.'

Wearily I could only mumble, 'Anything else.'

A smile crossed her face, 'You haven't asked me about the Monkey Run.'

'The what!'

'Every weekend the boys and girls used to parade up and down the hill all dressed in their best. Usually lads on one side and girls on the other. Give a lad the eye and maybe he'd turn back. Next week a tuppenny seat on the back row of the Premier. That's how I met my husband. Smart chap he was.' With these words her eyes closed but the smile remained.

As I left I began to wonder. People do romance at times and yet maybe Cheetham Hill was like that...before television.

Biographies

Kathleen Bohannon

I am 58 years old, married with two children and four grandchildren. My husband and I are both retired now. I love reading local history books and biographies. Since joining a writers' circle, I have enjoyed writing book reviews, poetry, and a collection of short stories about some of the Farnworth people I have known.

I have lived in Farnworth all my life, and I love the people of our town. Especially our senior citizens, who seem to have a dignity and kindness all their own.

John Clare

I first started writing when I was five. Progress has been steady. At 59 I am now able to cope with big words! Other interests include voluntary social work, reciting Stanley Holloway monologues at folk clubs, local history and singing in a male voice choir. My vices are too numerous to mention!

Ken Craven

I was born in 1945, and spent the early part of my childhood in Hulme, before moving to Old

Trafford where I attended the secondary modern school.

I worked in Trafford Park for ten years, then had several other jobs before giving up work in 1979 to look after our son when my wife resumed her teaching career. Since then I have had poems and articles published in 'Lancashire Life'; short stories broadcast on Radio Manchester; and a poem featured on BBC TV's North West Tonight.

I am a member of the Bury Writers' Group.

Harry Crossley

I was born in 1932 — the depression years — in Oldham, a typical Lancashire cotton mill town.

I left school at the age of fourteen, then joining the Navy served nine years.

After that came a succession of jobs until forming my own company with a colleague eighteen years ago, at which I've worked ever since.

I found literature late in life, well into my thirties, and became interested in writing but had to let it go to concentrate on the business. I have recently been able to gradually pick it up again.

Nell Harwood

Born in Oldham 61 years ago, I am married and have one son and three grandchildren. I have for many years been interested in the theatre, and

I am an active member of an amateur theatre group in Oldham.

I didn't start writing (apart from a little private scribbling for my eyes only) until I retired. I joined a creative writing class and later joined the 'Wordsmiths' group in Shaw, and went on from there.

I keep writing because I enjoy it, I can't think of a better reason than that.

Alrene Hughes

I was born and brought up in Northern Ireland and moved to Manchester in the late sixties. I now live in Bury with my husband and two small sons and work part-time for the BBC. I started writing about a year ago when I joined a local creative writing class and haven't stopped since!

Mary James

I am 53 years old. Married to a postman and mother of two lovely daughters aged 30 and 24. Also grandmother to a four year old scallywag named Thomas.

I was educated at a local convent grammar school but left at fifteen before taking 'O' levels. Currently making up for this omission and enjoying every minute of it!

Chequered working career, church cleaner, private secretary, playgroup organiser, physiotherapy aid, marriage guidance counsellor etc.

I have lived in Bury all my life and treasure the place and its warm loveable people, but I love travelling to other countries and meeting other people also.

Although ideas of writing have gone through my mind for many years, only recently, now liberated from so much domestic routine, have I really put pen to paper in earnest. I find it a very enjoyable pastime.

Heather Leach

I was born in 1943 and have lived in Manchester almost all my life. We moved to Wythenshawe in 1950 and I lived there until leaving home when I was nineteen. I left school at sixteen and have had a variety of jobs. For the last twelve years I have worked in Wythenshawe, as a community worker. I have three grown up children, one still at home, and I now live in Chorlton.

I have been writing since I was very young, but never thought it was 'real' writing. I recently joined a women writers' group who gave me a great deal of support and encouragement.

Elsie Maskell

I am aged 71 and I live in Manchester. I was born in Bangor, North Wales, of English parents, I moved to Cheshire at a very early age and then to Salford after the death of my mother, residing there until I married and went to live in Stratford-upon-Avon.

I have three married children, eight grandchildren and one great grandson. At this time I attend Commonword workshops twice a week, and am at present studying for my English GCSE examination.

My other interests apart from writing are music, politics and charity work.

Joy Openshaw

I was born, Joy Maddison, in 1931, and have lived in the Walkden area all my life.

I was educated at Walkden Moor Methodist Day School and Walkden Birch Road Secondary Modern School where I have been teacher-in-charge of commercial subjects since 1974.

I trained as a secretary at Worsley Technical College and was senior shorthand typist for the Worsley Urban District Council until 1956, when I left to have my three sons.

In 1964, I qualified as a teacher at Bolton Technical Teachers Training College and obtained a Bachelor of Arts Degree from the Open University in 1976.

My hobbies include researching local history, singing in the local Methodist church choir and Walkden High School staff choir, playing the organ, local Groundwork Trust, wildlife and creating pressed flower cards.

I am also a member of the local pressure group which is endeavouring to create a country park on Walkden Linnyshaw Moss.

John Rankle

I was brought up in what was a rural part of Chadderton, now regretfully annexed by bordering Oldham.

Foxdenton Lane was a pleasant meandering lane that led through gardens and meadows to thirteenth century Foxdenton Hall. As a boy I was proud to be a Foxyite and looking back I realised I'd had a very happy childhood with an elder brother and four sisters. Foxdenton Hall with its association with Cavaliers and Roundheads was ever a source of interest to myself and my pals. It also inspired me to write an essay which drew commendable praise from my school teacher. Writing was ever my favourite subject at school although I never allowed it to interfere with my sporting activities. My love of words, however, led to me writing a long poem which I signed with a *nom de plume* and sent it to the local newspaper. To my genuine amazement it was published and although I was thrilled I was also happy at being unrecognised as the author.

Ron Redshaw

I was born in 1943, one of eight children. At the age of fifteen I was sent to work in the local cotton mill. I began work at 7 am and finished at 6 pm. For a fifteen year old to work such hours was against the law, but the law was never there to check, so it was conveniently overlooked.

In 1959 at the age of sixteen I joined the Teddy boy brigade, or as the adults called us, the 'Edwardian Youths'.

From 1959 to 1981 I held down fifteen jobs. I married in 1963 and had three lovely daughters who have all since grown up and flown the nest. In 1981 I was made redundant and have been so to this day. I have always lived in Salford except for a brief period in my childhood when my mother and father decided to move to Little Hulton.

I have been writing since I was about sixteen years old but only seriously for the last four years. I love to write, it's what I want to do now, and I hope one day to make it my living.

Maureen Tottoh

I am a 47 year old single woman, and work full-time as a medical secretary in a group practice. Since my two daughters moved away from home — one is a student nurse, the other at university — I have lived alone.

Although I was brought up in Middleton Junction, I have lived in South Manchester for the past ten years.

I first started writing about six years ago when I joined a creative writing class at the College of Adult Education. This is my first attempt at getting my work published.

About Commonword

Commonword is a non-profitmaking community publishing co-operative, producing books by writers in the North West, and supporting and developing their work. In this way Commonword brings new writing to a wide audience.

Over a period of ten years Commonword has published poetry, short stories and other forms of creative writing. *Now Then* is the fourth title to be published under the **Crocus** imprint. Forthcoming books include *Talkers Through Dream Doors*, a collection of poetry and short stories by Black women writers, and *No Earthly Reason?* a volume of poetry about the environment.

In general, Commonword seeks to encourage the creative writing and publishing of the diverse groups in society who have lacked, or been excluded from, the means of expression through the written word. Working class writers, black writers, women, and lesbians and gay men all too often fall into this category.

To give writers the opportunity to develop their work in an informal setting, Commonword offers a variety of writers' workshops, such as Womanswrite, the Monday Night Group, and Northern Gay Writers.

Cultureword which is a part of Commonword,

and which acts as a focus for Asian and Afro-Caribbean writers, organises the Identity Writers' Workshop. Cultureword also co-ordinates 'Identity' magazine, and a writing competition for Black writers.

In addition to writers' workshops and publishing, Commonword offers a manuscript reading service to give constructive criticism, and can give information and advice to writers about facilities in their immediate locality. 'Writers Reign' magazine contains both information and new writing.

Commonword is supported by: the Association of Greater Manchester Authorities, North West Arts and Manchester Education Committee.

The Commonword/Cultureword offices are at Cheetwood House, 21 Newton Street, Piccadilly, Manchester. Our phone number is (061) 236 2773. We would like to hear from you.

If you've enjoyed reading Now Then, why not try some of our other recent books?

She Says

She Says is a new collection from five women writers celebrating the vitality and variety of women's poetry today. Pat Amick writes movingly and skilfully about her feelings for her father, of childhood joys and of the bitter-sweet nature of romance. Cathy Bolton's work deals with relationships, and the way in which they are constantly cut across by questions of power, the past and sexuality. Anne Paley's poetry has a searching and reflective quality, whilst describing situations that affect many women. Sheila Parry uses powerful images, culled from folklore, myths and fairytales, in her work, whilst Cath Staincliffe expresses her thoughts about love, motherhood and politics in a way that is always challenging and original.

"This collection of poems is rich and varied in form and content and always thought provoking. Read it." (7 DAYS)

£2.95   96 pages   ISBN 0 946745 50 1

Black and Priceless

Black and Priceless is an exciting collection of poetry and short stories by Black writers. The skill of Asian women's writing is illustrated by the work of Deepa Banerjee and Debjani Chatterjee, whilst in Peter Kalu's 'The Adventures of Maud Mellington', we have a hilarious detective story with a difference. The poetry of John Lyons tells with passion and energy of the experience of living with racism in this country, whilst Sally Neaser writes movingly of her feelings about motherhood. This selection of twenty-one writers includes those who are fast becoming familiar names, alongside others for whom this book represents their debut in print. A highly readable and diverse collection, *Black and Priceless* reflects the power of Black ink!

''All the pieces in this work have a positive strength, and the direct use of language is raw and powerful ... **Black and Priceless** is a timely eruption of a new and expressive black conciousness.'' (City Life)

£3.50   200 pages   ISBN 0 946745 45 5

Holding Out: Short Stories by Women

Holding Out contains a compelling and challenging selection of writing. With both humour and pathos, this collection vividly portrays women's lives. The stories in the book take the reader from a still birth in 1930's Lancashire in 'The Confinement', through to a disturbing tale of child sex abuse in 1980's Britain in 'Daddy's Toy'. 'A Pair of Jeans' describes how what may appear to be a simple item of clothing can wreak havoc in the life of an Asian family, whilst 'Nothing Happened' is an affectionately wry look at life on the dole. These are just a small selection from this collection of twenty-one stories, which demonstrates both the strength, and the variety, of contemporary women's writing.

"This impressive collection of new work is sincere and honest, and it's enjoyable because the women featured cope with their lives with strength, courage and most of all, humour." (CITY LIFE)

£3.50   56 pages   ISBN 0 946745 30 7

Poetic Licence

Poetic Licence is an exuberant and bubbling brew of poetry from a diversity of poets living and working in Greater Manchester. Their work celebrates the many pleasures of poetry from the serious and intense, to the playful and humorous. This book contains work from some exciting new poets. There's writing from the Black Writers' Workshop, and Northern Gay Writers, as well as from 'Chances' — a group of disabled and able-bodied writers, and performance poetry from Stand and Deliver. Peter

Street writes movingly of old age and disability, whilst Anne Paley looks at life in the '80s as a woman, there's poetry in patwa from Patrick Elly, and short witty pieces from Gary Boswell.

"There are many different emotions and moods to be found within these pages and, read in its entirety, the whole volume is disarmingly powerful...Excellent value for money." (CITY LIFE)

£2.50   208 pages   ISBN 0 946745 40 4

Between Mondays

The Monday Night Group

This collection of poetry is the latest book from Commonword's Monday Night Group. It brings together some promising new writers with plenty to say about life in the city, sexuality, Catholicism and many other subjects.'A Northerner's Nightmare' describes the horror of a Salford lad lost on the London tube; 'Asleep in The Afternoon' takes us back to schooldays; 'Sideshow Sexuality' compares an adolescent girl's experience with the life of the fairground. This is just a small selection from a wide ranging anthology, which stretches from ranting to romance and from childhood to old age.

"By publishing this book, Commonword has encouraged writers who might not otherwise put pen to paper, who have valuable lives to share with us." (ARTFUL REPORTER)

£2.50   104 pages   ISBN 0 946745 35 8

Autobiography

Australian Journal: Alf Ironmonger   60p
In 1946, off the coast of South Australia, two
young shipmates decide to jump ashore. This is
their tale...
ISBN 0 946745 01 3   64 pages

Dobroyed: Leslie Wilson   £1.20
The unique inside story of one person's ex-
perience of a year spent in an approved school.
ISBN 0 950599 74 3   142 pages

Fiction

Marshall's Big Score: John Gowling   £1.20
A book about a love affair, played out against
the backdrop of the gay scene in London, Liver-
pool and Manchester.
ISBN 0 946745 03 X   76 pages

Turning Points: Northern Gay Writers £2.95

This collection of short stories and poetry explores   moments   of   crisis   —   turning
points — in the lives of a variety of characters,
with various different conclusions...
ISBN 0 946745 20 X   120 pages

Poetry

Liberation Soldier: Joe Smythe £2.50
Employing a variety of styles, Joe explores the
discontents and disturbances of the times, from
inner city riots to apartheid in South Africa.
ISBN 0 946745 25 0   84 pages

Hermit Crab: Di Williams 30p
Using the imagery of the sea and the seashore,
these poems tell of a daughter's journey towards
independence.
ISBN 0 946745 15 3   28 pages

Consider Only This: Sarah Ward 30p
A selection of poems which captures the atmosphere of moorland, cotton mills and small
town life.
ISBN 0 946745 04 8 28 pages

Diary of A Divorce: Wendy Whitfield £1.00
Wendy Whitfield reflects on the breakdown of
her marriage in a series of poems and cartoons.
ISBN 0 9505997 7 8   28 pages

Forthcoming Titles

Talkers Through Dream Doors £3.50
A new collection of poetry and short stories by
Asian and Afro-Caribbean women writers.
ISBN 0 946745 60 9   Publication date: 1 June
1989

No Earthly Reason? £3.50
A poetry anthology looking at the environment
and how it affects us all — from the world on
the doorstep to global issues!
ISBN 0 946745 65 X   Publication date:
10 October 1989

Relative to me... £3.95
Families — love 'em or hate 'em, this book of
short stories will both move and delight you.
ISBN 0 946745 70 6 Publication date: 14
February 1990

ORDER FORM

TITLE	QTY.	PRICE	AMOUNT
She Says		£2.95	. . . . . .
Black and Priceless		£3.50	. . . . . .
Holding Out		£3.50	. . . . . .
Poetic Licence		£2.50	. . . . . .
Between Mondays		£2.50	. . . . . .
Liberation Soldier		£2.50	. . . . . .
Turning Points		£2.95	. . . . . .
Hermit Crab		£0.30	. . . . . .
Consider Only This		£0.30	. . . . . .
Marshall's Big Score		£1.20	. . . . . .
Dobroyed		£1.20	. . . . . .
Australian Journal		£0.60	. . . . . .
Diary of A Divorce		£1.00	. . . . . .
Talkers Through Dream Doors		£3.50	. . . . . .
No Earthly Reason?		£3.50	. . . . . .
Relative to me...		£3.95	. . . . . .

TOTAL   . . . . . .

Please send a cheque or postal order, made payable to Commonword Ltd, covering the purchase price plus 25p per book postage and packing.

NAME: . . . .

ADDRESS: . . . .

. . . .

. . . . Postcode . . . .

Please return to: Commonword, Cheetwood House, 21 Newton Street, Manchester M1 1FZ.